101

ESSENTIAL TIPS

Cro

101
ESSENTIAL TIPS

Crochet

Produced for DK by
Sands Publishing Solutions
4 Jenner Way, Eccles, Aylesford, Kent ME20 7SQ

Editorial Partners   David & Sylvia Tombesi-Walton
Design Partner   Simon Murrell

Senior Editor   Chauney Dunford
Senior Art Editor   Elaine Hewson
Managing Editor   Penny Warren
Jacket Designer   Kathryn Wilding
Senior Pre-production Producer   Tony Phipps
Senior Producer   Ché Creasey
Art Director   Jane Bull
Publisher   Mary Ling

Written by   Lucy Horne

First published in Great Britain in 2015 by
Dorling Kindersley Limited, 80 Strand, London WC2R 0RL

A Penguin Random House Company

2 4 6 8 10 9 7 5 3

004–274508–May/2015

A CIP catalogue record for this book is available from the British Library.

ISBN 978-0-2410-1472-1

Printed and bound in China

A WORLD OF IDEAS:
SEE ALL THERE IS TO KNOW

www.dk.com

101 ESSENTIAL TIPS

EQUIPMENT & YARN

1 WHAT IS CROCHET?

Crochet is an easy way to make fabrics from yarn. The results are similar to knitting, though the techniques and tools used are very different. In fact, crochet is simple to learn, since every stitch is based on the same principle. It is also versatile, allowing you to make a wide range of items from many materials. Projects are often small enough to be very portable, so you can take them with you for when you get a spare moment. You will soon be creating all kinds of fabulous things for you and your friends.

2 WHAT CAN YOU MAKE?

The only limit is your imagination. You can make lacy scarves and warm pullovers, toys for your children, and cushions for your home. It is very rewarding to cosy up on a cold winter's day under a beautiful blanket that you have crocheted yourself. Once you master the skill, you can follow patterns or create your own – the possibilities are endless.

Toys

Bedding

Bags

Clothing

TYPES OF HOOK

3 Most crochet hooks are a similar shape, but they come in many different materials. Which type you use is up to you. Some people prefer the warm feel of wood or bamboo; others prefer the cheaper metal ones – try various types to find your favourite. Hooks are available from most wool and craft shops and can also be bought online. Whichever type you choose, remember it is the size of the hook that matters.

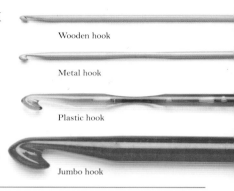

Wooden hook

Metal hook

Plastic hook

Jumbo hook

HOOK SIZE CONVERSION CHART		
Metric	**US size**	**Old UK**
0.6mm	14 steel	
0.75mm	12 steel	
1mm	11 steel	
1.25mm	7 steel	
1.5mm	6 steel	
1.75mm	5 steel	
2mm		14
2.25mm	B-1	
2.5mm		12
2.75mm	c-2	
3mm		10
3.25mm	D-3	
3.5mm	E-4	9
3.75mm	F-5	
4mm	G-6	8
4.5mm	7	7
5mm	H-8	6
5.5mm	I-9	5
6mm	J-10	4
6.5mm	K-10½	3
7mm		2
8mm	L-11	
9mm	M-13	
10mm	N-15	
12mm	P	
15mm	Q (16mm)	
20mm	S (19mm)	

HOOK SIZES

4 In the UK, crochet hooks are sized in millimetres, but you may find old patterns that use the previous hook sizes or an American pattern with US hook sizes. This chart (left) offers an easy way to convert the US and old British sizes to the metric system.

WHY SIZE OF HOOK MATTERS

5 A hook's size is the diameter of its shank (see Tip 6), and it is this that determines the size of the stitches. Most yarn-ball information and patterns will tell you which hook to use, but you will soon come to know which size works best with which yarn. If you want a tighter, closer stitched result, you can use a slightly smaller hook; for a looser weave, use a larger hook. (For more on this, see Tip 20.) Eventually you will amass a collection of different-sized hooks to enable you to work with any type of yarn.

6 HOLDING YOUR HOOK

The two most common hook holds are shown below, but there is no right or wrong way to hold a crochet hook, other than with a light grip and in your dominant hand. It is more important that you feel comfortable, that there is no stress on your fingers or wrist, and that you are able to control the yarn tension. You may even find that you change your hold depending on the size of your hook.

Hook tip

Throat   *Shank*

Hook lip   *Thumb rest*   *Handle*

7 KNIFE HOLD

In this hold you grasp the hook as you would a knife when cutting food. This hold is often easiest when crocheting with very chunky yarn and using a jumbo hook, since it gives more grip for pulling very thick yarn through itself. Don't hold the hook too close to the tip; use your fingers along the hook to control it.

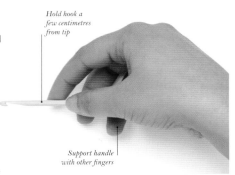

Hold hook a few centimetres from tip

Support handle with other fingers

8 PEN HOLD

In this hold, take the hook as though it is a pen you are about to write with. Some hooks even have a thumb rest so that you place your fingers the right distance from the tip. The handle sits between your thumb and forefinger. This hold is particularly useful with smaller hooks and delicate yarns.

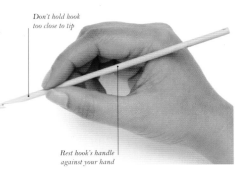

Don't hold hook too close to tip

Rest hook's handle against your hand

9 CARE OF YOUR HOOKS

A purpose-made hook roll can protect your hooks from damage and allow you to see them all clearly when selecting one. Wooden hooks may need occasional treatment with linseed oil, while metal or plastic hooks will sometimes need wiping with a damp cloth to keep them clean and free from grease.

HOLDING IT TOGETHER
Use a bag to store your ongoing projects, so that all you need is kept together in one place and portable.

10 OTHER EQUIPMENT

As well as your hook and yarn, you will need some other basic, inexpensive equipment. Scissors are used to cut yarn as you finish with it; stitch markers will help you keep track, especially when working in rounds; blunt-ended yarn needles are for sewing in ends or seams; and a tape measure to ensure your work is the right size.

Yarn bobbins

Row counter

Stitch markers

Scissors

Blunt-ended yarn needles

Tape measure

Pins and pincushion

YARN TYPES

11

You can crochet with almost anything that can be drawn into a long strip, but using the right yarn is vital for getting the effect you want. Think about what you are making: what will it be used for? How should it look when finished? Consider whether it will need to be washed regularly. All these things will inform your choice of yarn.

Versatile yarn; soft and smooth to work with

Lightweight cotton

Warm and hard-wearing; needs careful washing

Wool

Easy to work with; ideal for baby clothes

Fuzzy yarn for winter items; soft, warm, and light

Fine cotton

Alpaca

Strong, with slight sheen; holds its shape well

Mercerized cotton

Luxurious and expensive; lovely to work with

Cashmere

Very fine; usually used for lace and filet crochet

Beautiful yarn with soft sheen; for special occasions

Cotton crochet thread

NATURAL FIBRES

Natural fibres come from plants or animals. They are lovely to crochet with and come in a wide range of weights and colours. They work well for clothing because they are breathable, but they tend to be expensive. Also, the finished items can be hard to care for, because natural fibres often shrink when washed.

Silk

Gives good stitch definition; works best with open stitches

Tape yarn

Soft and strong; easy to use and to care for

Wool and cotton mixes

Gives interesting and colourful results

Plied yarn

Lightweight and strong; washes well and is hard-wearing

Nylon

Can be scratchy against skin, so best for trims

Metallic yarn

Light and soft; great for making bulky lightweight items

Strong combination yarn

Natural & synthetic mix

Cheap to buy; available in many bright colours

Acrylic

Spun yarn

SYNTHETIC FIBRES & YARN BLENDS

Synthetic fibres are often cheaper and more durable than natural fibres, but they are not as soft or as warm. Consequently, they are often used in blends to make natural fibres stronger and easier to care for.

SPECIALITY YARNS

There is a huge range of speciality yarns that can add sparkle or texture to your crochet. Smooth yarns are great for intricate stitches because they show the detail, while bulky yarns make quick work of larger items.

12 WHAT TO LOOK FOR WHEN CHOOSING YARN

When buying yarn for a project, always bear in mind a couple of questions: what are you making, and who is it for? Knowing the answers to these questions will help you choose a suitable weight and fibre content of the yarn. Bear in mind how much use it will get and how washable it needs to be – a soft scarf will require different yarn from a hard-wearing toy, for example. Think about the practical uses for the finished item, and consider the personality of the recipient.

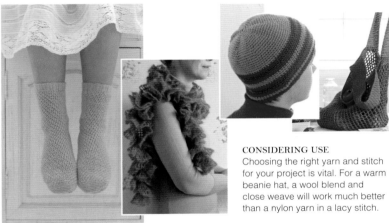

CONSIDERING USE

Choosing the right yarn and stitch for your project is vital. For a warm beanie hat, a wool blend and close weave will work much better than a nylon yarn in a lacy stitch.

PACKAGING

Yarn is packaged in several ways. Doughnuts and balls comprise yarn that is wound around itself. The working end usually comes from the centre, allowing you to keep the ballband in place to stop the yarn unravelling. A hank, or skein, contains yarn that is twisted, which prevents it from unravelling in transit. Before you can crochet with a hank, you must wind it into a ball.

Doughnut

Ball

Hank, or skein

13

BALLBAND INFORMATION

The information on the band around your yarn tells you everything you need to know: what size hook to use, what the tension (see Tip 19) should be, and how to wash and care for it. It also says what it's made from, how much is in the ball, what colour it is, and which dye lot it is from. Use yarn from the same dye lot to ensure there's no variation in tone.

BAND SYMBOLS

These are some of the symbols you will find on a ballband. They will help you select the right yarn for your project.

22 ss / 10cm / 28 rows / 10cm	**151**	**420**
Tension	Dye lot number	Shade/colour
4mm (UK 8/ US G-6)	100% **WOOL**	2	**40g**
Recommended crochet hook size	Fibre content	Yarn weight and thickness	Weight of ball, doughnut, or hank

14

DRAPE

Once you know what you are making and which yarn to use, think about how the fabric will feel and drape when finished. A solid, stiff crocheted fabric would be uncomfortable for clothing but great for toys. You can adjust drape by changing the stitch or hook size to create tighter or looser fabric.

THINK ABOUT THE ITEM

Consider yarn type, hook size, and stitch when thinking about how a finished piece will flow and drape. The longer and lacier the stitch, the more it will drape.

15 YARN WEIGHT NAMES

Now that we all live in a global marketplace, you may find yourself using foreign patterns or buying yarn from abroad. Crochet has a huge following in the United States, and there is a lot of information online using American terminology. The standard weight system numbers yarn from 0 to 6 based on its weight, or thickness. The chart below will help you convert between different weight systems.

YARN WEIGHT CONVERSION CHART

Standard weight system	UK name	US name
0 or Lace	1-ply	Laceweight or thread
1 or Superfine	2-ply/3-ply	Baby, fingering, sock
2 or Fine	4-ply	Sport
3 or Light	Double knit (DK)	DK, light worsted
4 or Medium	Aran	Worsted, fisherman
5 or Bulky	Chunky	Bulky
6 or Super bulky	Super chunky	Super bulky, extra bulky

16 HOOK SIZE FOR YARN WEIGHT

There is usually a recommended hook size for each yarn weight identified on the yarn ballband or in the pattern, if you are using one. The chart below is a guideline to help you achieve the intended result. Experiment with different hook sizes to see how it changes the look and feel of your piece. You may, of course, opt to ignore the recommended hook size completely to achieve your own desired effect.

RECOMMENDED HOOK SIZE FOR YARN WEIGHT

Yarn weight	Recommended UK hook size
2-ply, lace, fingering	1.5mm, 1.75mm, 2mm, 2.25mm
3-ply, superfine, fingering, baby	2.75mm, 3mm, 3.25mm
4-ply, fine, sportweight, baby	3.25mm, 3.5mm, 3.75mm
Double knit (DK), light, worsted, 5–6-ply	3.75mm, 4mm, 4.5mm
Aran, medium, worsted, Afghan, 12-ply	5mm, 5.5mm
Chunky, bulky, craft, rug, 14-ply	6mm, 6.5mm, 7mm, 8mm
Super bulky, super chunky, bulky, roving, 16-ply and up	9mm, 10mm

17 RECYCLING YARN

Yarn can be expensive, so keep your costs down by recycling old yarn. Do you have any sweaters that you don't wear anymore? Unpick them, rewind the yarn, and you will be able to create something new without spending a penny. Reused yarn will have kinks in it from the old stitches; you can wash and dry the yarn once it's unpicked to help flatten it, but crocheting with kinked yarn rarely affects the new stitches.

SECONDHAND BARGAINS
Buy cheap knitwear in charity shops to recycle the yarn. Just check the washing instructions, and clean it before you crochet.

18 DEALING WITH KNOTS

As you crochet, you may come across knots in the yarn, where two pieces have been joined together. The best way to deal with a knot is to cut it out while you still have a long tail to work with. You can then treat it the same as joining a new ball of yarn: weave in the ends, or crochet over them with the rest of the yarn. To ensure you leave enough yarn before the knot to weave in, always pull as much yarn off the ball as you would need to complete a row.

SAY NO TO KNOTS!
It is quite common to find two pieces knotted together even in the most expensive yarns. Make sure you never crochet over them.

TENSION SWATCHES

Tension is the number of stitches and rows you need in a specific length and width of crocheted fabric. The pattern or yarn ballband will usually give you this information, and it is important to match it so that your finished item is the correct size. Before you start a project, make a tension swatch to check it matches the pattern requirements. Tension is affected by yarn weight, hook size, and your own crochet technique.

FINE-YARN TENSION

In fine yarns, it is harder to see the difference made by using different sizes of hook, but even these subtle variations will have an effect on the finished piece.

2mm hook   2.5mm hook   3mm hook

LIGHTWEIGHT-YARN TENSION

As you use slightly thicker yarn, such as double knit, the impact of larger hooks becomes more apparent. The larger the hook, the softer the fabric texture.

2.5mm hook   4mm hook   4.5mm hook

BULKY-YARN TENSION

The change in tension by using different hook sizes can also create different effects. The pattern will tell you how tight your tension should be.

6mm hook   7mm hook   8mm hook

CHANGING TENSION

You can check tension by making a swatch of the number of stitches suggested by the pattern and measuring its length and width to see if it matches the pattern tension. If it is too small, try again with the next hook size up; if too big, go down a size. Never change tension by trying to crochet tighter or looser – change the hook, not your technique.

21 OTHER THINGS TO CROCHET WITH

You can crochet with anything that can be drawn into a long strip. This means you can experiment with different materials to create all kinds of things. Use a large hook with thicker materials to form very stiff fabrics that can be used to make household objects, or use a small hook with thinner materials for delicate jewellery and tiny projects. Look in hardware stores and garden centres for unusual things to crochet with, and let your creativity run wild.

STRING

This hard-wearing, versatile medium can be used for all kinds of objects in various colours, such as cushions, bowls, and doormats.

FABRIC

Old T-shirts can be cut into strips and knotted together to make a thick yarn ideal for rugs, pet beds, and pouffes, for example.

PLASTIC BAGS

Cut up plastic bags and string them together, then work them into waterproof garden-seat pads, door mats, or stronger shopping bags.

WIRE

Crocheting with wire can be hard on your hands, so it is best suited to small projects such as bracelets and necklaces.

PATTERNS & CHARTS

22 WHERE TO FIND PATTERNS

Books and printed patterns can be bought in wool and craft shops, but the internet is a great resource, too, especially for free patterns. The international crochet community is also very generous when it comes to sharing ideas and information. Crocheting friends swap and share patterns, and there are even smartphone apps that offer access to a database of designs for anything you may want to make. Just be aware of any copyright restrictions that may forbid you from sharing patterns or selling finished items from someone else's pattern.

23 TERMINOLOGY & ABBREVIATIONS

Crochet uses its own specific language. This jargon is easy to learn and helps make patterns easier to understand, but there are some differences between the UK and US versions. It is important to know this, in case you find yourself using a pattern written in American terminology. This chart gives the basic stitch names in both UK and US terminology, as well as their abbreviations, to help you translate American crochet patterns.

STITCH TERMS & ABBREVIATIONS

UK/US	UK term	US term
dc / sc	double crochet	single crochet
htr / hdc	half treble crochet	half double crochet
tr / dc	treble crochet	double crochet
dtr / tr	double treble crochet	treble crochet
trtr / dtr	triple treble crochet	double treble crochet
qtr / trtr	quadruple treble crochet	triple treble crochet
quintr / quadtr	quintuple treble crochet	quadruple treble crochet
2 dc in same st / 2 sc in same st	two-stitch dc increase	two-stitch sc increase
3 dc in same st / 3 sc in same st	three-stitch dc increase	three-stitch sc increase
dc2tog / sc2tog	double crochet two together	single crochet two together
dc3tog / sc3tog	double crochet three together	single crochet three together
fptr / fpdc	front post treble crochet	front post double crochet
bptr / bpdc	back post treble crochet	back post double crochet

HOW TO READ A PATTERN

To simplify instructions in a crochet pattern, only basic terminology is used, and it is often abbreviated to save space. It is fairly straightforward to learn, and you will quickly become fluent in it. Crochet patterns are usually set out by numbering each row to be crocheted and giving the instructions per row. This allows you to keep track of where you are in a pattern simply by counting how many rows you have crocheted. The chart below includes some of the most common pattern abbreviations.

PATTERN ABBREVIATIONS

Abbreviation	Meaning
alt	alternate
beg	beginning
bet	between
blo	back loop only
CC	contrasting colour
ch	chain stitch
ch-sp	chain space
CL	cluster
cm	centimetres
cont	continue
dec	decrease
flo	front loop only
foll	follow
inc	increase
mm	millimetres
patt / patts	pattern / patterns
rem	remaining
rep	repeat
RS	right side
sp	space(s)
ss	slip stitch
st / sts	stitch / stitches
t-ch	turning chain
tbl	through back loop (alternative term for back loop only)
tfl	through front loop (alternative term for front loop only)
tog	together
WS	wrong side
yrh (yo in the US)	yarn round hook (yarn over)
() or ☐	work instructions within the parentheses as many times as shown – for example, ()2 times
*	work instructions marked with asterisks as many times as shown

CHART SYMBOLS

Some crochet patterns are written in the form of a chart made of symbols, showing where each stitch goes. These charts are read row by row, back and forth, or in a spiral. Symbols are not universal, so check the pattern's key before you start working on a project.

BASIC STITCHES

These are basic stitch symbols. They show the heights of the stitches, while the base points to the space into which it is worked.

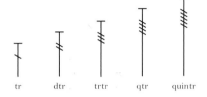

| ch | ss | dc | htr | tr | dtr | trtr | qtr | quintr |

SPECIAL STITCHES & STITCH COMBINATIONS

These symbols show special stitches such as picots and post stitches, as well as stitch increases and decreases. Again, the base of each symbol shows the stitch or chain into which it is to be worked.

3-ch, 4-ch, 5-ch picots   fptr   bptr   dc2tog   dc3tog   htr2tog   htr3tog

tr2tog   tr3tog   2dc in same st   3dc in same st   2htr in same st   3htr in same st

SHELLS, CLUSTERS, BOBBLES & POPCORNS

These symbols show where stitches are worked together for a specific effect. A visual representation of each stitch in the combination makes it easier to see how the stitch is constructed.

3-, 4-, 5-tr bobbles

2-, 3-, 4-, 5-, 6-tr shells

2-, 3-, 4-, 5-, 6-tr clusters

3-, 4-, 5-tr popcorns

HOW TO READ A CHART

26 The chart below is an exact visual representation of the piece of crochet pictured. You start at the bottom of the chart and follow the direction upwards, just as you crochet. At the bottom of the page is the same pattern in written form, to demonstrate how each system works.

Row 4

Row 2

Row 3

Foundation chain starts here

Row 1

Close shell stitch

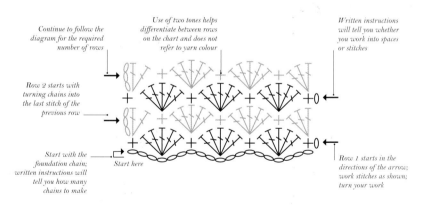

Continue to follow the diagram for the required number of rows

Use of two tones helps differentiate between rows on the chart and does not refer to yarn colour

Written instructions will tell you whether you work into spaces or stitches

Row 2 starts with turning chains into the last stitch of the previous row

Start with the foundation chain; written instructions will tell you how many chains to make

Start here

Row 1 starts in the directions of the arrow; work stitches as shown; turn your work

WRITTEN INSTRUCTIONS

Work a chain that is a multiple of 6, and add two chains.

Row 1: 1 dc in 2nd ch from hook, *miss next 2 ch, 5 tr in next ch, miss next 2 ch, 1 dc in next ch; rep from * to end, turn.

Row 2: ch 3 (counts as first tr), 2 tr in first dc, *miss next 2 tr, 1 dc in next tr, 5 tr in next dc (between shells); rep from *, ending last rep with 3 tr in last dc, turn.

Row 3: ch 1 (does not count as first stitch), 1 dc in first tr, *5 tr in next dc (between shells), miss next 2 tr, 1 dc in next tr; rep from *, work last dc in top of 3-ch at end, turn.

Rep rows 2 and 3 to required length.

GETTING STARTED

27 HOLDING THE YARN

To control its tension, you need to know how best to hold the yarn. Take the hook in your dominant hand and the yarn in the other; this hand controls the tension and prevents the yarn from tangling as you work. As with the hook, there is no right or wrong way to hold the yarn, but the two most commonly used methods are shown below.

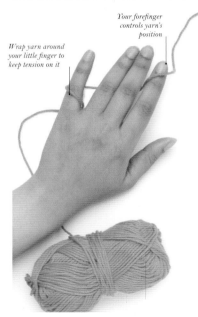

Wrap yarn around your little finger to keep tension on it

Your forefinger controls yarn's position

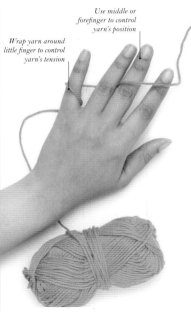

Wrap yarn around little finger to control yarn's tension

Use middle or forefinger to control yarn's position

METHOD 1
The end of the yarn closest to the ball goes around your little finger, under your middle fingers, and over your forefinger. You use your forefinger to position the yarn.

METHOD 2
Wrap the end of the yarn around your little finger, under the ring finger, and over the next two fingers. Use either the index or middle finger to position the yarn.

28 LEFT-HANDED CROCHETERS

Most patterns need to be adjusted for left-handers. When following a garment pattern, remember that a right front section, for example, will be your left front section. When following a chart, you must start on the left; you could photograph the chart and flip it on your computer.

29 RIGHT-HANDED CROCHETERS

Right-handed crocheters work from right to left and follow charts the same way. If a right-handed crocheter is teaching a left-handed crocheter, they just need to sit opposite each other, so the left-handed person can simply copy exactly what the right-handed person is doing.

30 CONTROLLING TENSION AS YOU WORK

The hand that holds the yarn also holds the crochet as it comes off your hook. The tension on the yarn only needs to be enough to keep it taut, so you can easily pick it up with the hook. Do not hold the yarn too tight, since it will be harder to work with, and your stitches will be small and uneven; but if you hold it too loose, you will get in a tangle and have floppy stitches.

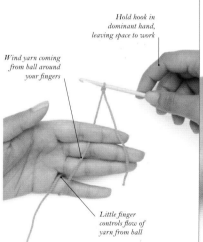

Wind yarn coming from ball around your fingers

Hold hook in dominant hand, leaving space to work

Little finger controls flow of yarn from ball

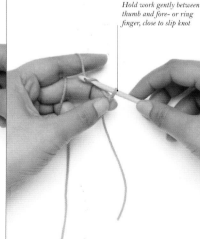

Hold work gently between thumb and fore- or ring finger, close to slip knot

1 Put your yarn on the hook with a slip knot (see Tip 31), and hold the working end in the other hand, anchoring it around your little finger. This readies the yarn for you to work it.

2 Use your thumb and forefinger or ring finger to hold the crochet as it comes off your hook. Hold the yarn up for the hook with your forefinger or middle finger.

MAKING A SLIP KNOT

31

The first step in any crochet work is to attach your yarn to your hook. This is done with a slip knot, which also forms the first loop you work through. With only a little practice, slip knots quickly become very easy to do. You can make a slip knot around your fingers and put it on the hook, or you can create it using the hook, as show here.

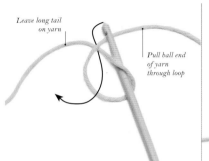

Leave long tail on yarn

Pull ball end of yarn through loop

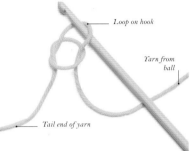

Loop on hook

Yarn from ball

Tail end of yarn

1 Make a loop with the ball end of the yarn over the tail end. Put your hook through the loop, catch the ball end of the yarn, and pull it back through the loop.

2 You now have a loop on the hook and a loose knot below it. Leave a long tail (12–15cm [5–6in]) since you must weave this end in when you have finished your piece.

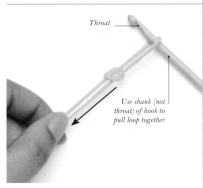

Throat

Use shank (not throat) of hook to pull loop together

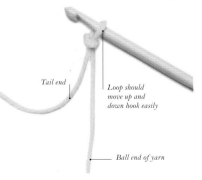

Tail end

Loop should move up and down hook easily

Ball end of yarn

3 Pull on the ends of the yarn to tighten it a little around your hook. However, do not pull it too tight, because you need to work your hook into this loop.

4 The loop should move freely up and down your hook but not slide off the end. You can loosen it by pulling the ball end of the yarn, and tighten it by pulling the tail end.

32 MAKING A FOUNDATION CHAIN

The foundation chain is the point from which your crochet grows. Make sure you keep it even and not so tight that you won't be able to insert the hook through the loops later. The number of stitches in your foundation chain depends on how wide your work will be. Most patterns advise how many foundation chains to make.

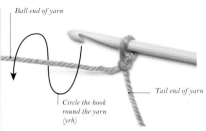

Ball end of yarn

Circle the hook round the yarn (yrh)

Tail end of yarn

1 Despite the term "yarn round hook" (or "yarn over"), you actually move the hook anticlockwise around the yarn from the ball.

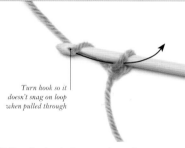

Turn hook so it doesn't snag on loop when pulled through

2 Turn the hook downwards so the yarn catches under the lip, then pull it smoothly through the loop on the hook.

First chain stitch

3 Keep your chain stitches even and not too tight by forming a rhythm as you chain, always working into the loop on the hook.

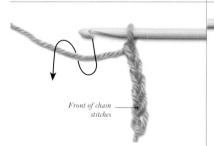

Front of chain stitches

4 Repeat steps 1 and 2 until you have as many chain stitches as you need. Aim to make stitches neat, even, and not too loose.

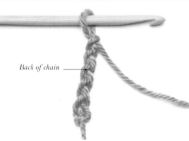

Back of chain

5 The front of a foundation chain shows a row of flat Vs, while the back is simply a row of raised bumps.

33 COUNTING CHAINS

Crochet requires you to count stitches often to ensure you are following the pattern correctly. Always count your chain stitches before you start to crochet your first row. If you don't have the right number of foundation chains, you won't have room to complete the stitches properly. Look at the front of the chain, and count the V shapes. Remember: the slip knot at the start and the loop on your hook do not count.

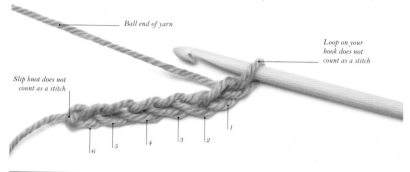

Ball end of yarn

Loop on your hook does not count as a stitch

Slip knot does not count as a stitch

6   5   4   3   2   1

34 WORKING INTO CHAINS

The foundation chain does not count as a row; it is simply the base for your work, and it can sometimes be difficult to crochet into it. It takes some practice, but once you have completed the first row into the foundation chain, the other rows will be easier. The front of your foundation chain shows each chain as a flat V shape; insert your hook under the top strand of the Vs to make stitches into the foundation chain.

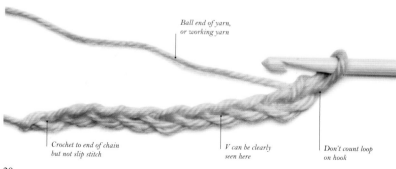

Ball end of yarn, or working yarn

Crochet to end of chain but not slip stitch

V can be clearly seen here

Don't count loop on hook

STITCHES

SLIP STITCH

35

Slip stitch is rarely used to create whole blocks of fabric, but it is important to learn because it is used to finish off rounds and join pieces together. A slip stitch does not add any real height to your work and would make a dense, unyielding fabric, which is why it is not one of the main crochet stitches.

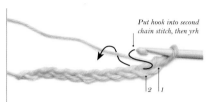

Put hook into second chain stitch, then yrh

1 Working into your foundation chain, insert the hook into the second chain from the hook. Wrap the yarn around the hook (yrh).

Loop on hook

2 Draw the loop back through the chain; you now have two loops on your hook. Pull the loop closest to the tip of the hook through the other loop.

Chain stitches stretch as you work into them

3 Continue across the foundation chain in the same way. It can be difficult to work slip stitches because they are so small, so aim to keep them fairly loose.

Make last slip stitch of row into last chain before turning

4 When you reach the end of the chain, turn the crochet around to look at the back of the work. Your hook should be at the right-hand edge (if you are right-handed).

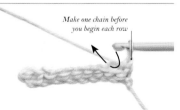

Make one chain before you begin each row

5 Start your next row by making a chain stitch (called a turning chain here). Continue to work slip stitches across in the top strand of the previous row of stitches.

36

DOUBLE CROCHET

Crochet is based around a few basic stitches that vary in height and give different finishes. Double crochet is the shortest stitch. It is easy to learn and worth practising until you feel comfortable with it, since it will make it easier to learn the other stitches. Double crochet creates a close, compact fabric that is very versatile. Once you have mastered it, you can make garments, toys, and household items with double crochet.

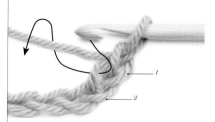

1 Make a foundation chain as long as you need the fabric to be wide. Insert your hook into the second chain from the hook. (The first chain acts as the turning chain.)

Hold base of chain as you pull yarn through

2 Yarn round hook (yrh), then, holding the base of the foundation chain between your thumb and forefinger, pull the loop back through the same chain stitch.

3 You now have two loops on your hook. Yrh again, gently using the hand that is holding the yarn to create an even tension. Do not pull the yarn too tight.

4 Draw the yarn through both loops on the hook. Try to make it a smooth movement. Turn the hook so the lip is facing downwards to prevent it from snagging on the loops.

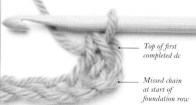

Top of first completed dc

Missed chain at start of foundation row

5 You have now completed your first double crochet (dc) stitch. Remember: the first chain is used as the turning chain, so do not include it when you count your stitches.

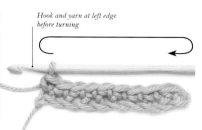

Hook and yarn at left edge before turning

6 Carry on working across your foundation chain, making one double crochet in each chain stitch. Crochet to the end of the foundation chain but not into the slip knot.

7 When you reach the end of the foundation chain, turn your work around so you begin the next row on the reverse side. Right-handers crochet right to left.

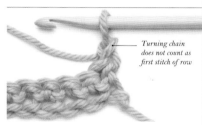

Turning chain does not count as first stitch of row

Put hook under both strands

8 Start the second row by making one chain to bring your work to the correct height for the next dc row. The edges of your piece will be crooked if you overlook this stage.

9 Continue the next row by making double crochet stitches under both strands of the V at the top of each stitch of the previous round.

Insert hook under both strands of top of last dc in previous row

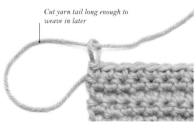

Cut yarn tail long enough to weave in later

10 At the end of the row, make sure you work your last dc into the last stitch of the previous row. You should have the same number of stitches in each row.

11 When you have finished your piece, cut off the yarn. Pull the loose end through the loop on your hook, remove the hook, then pull the yarn tail to close the loop.

HALF TREBLE CROCHET

37

Half treble crochet makes a softer, more flexible fabric than double crochet. It requires two chains at the start of the second and later rows to make your work the correct height. The first stitch of each row after the turning chain is worked into the second half treble of the previous row. Unlike in double crochet, the turning chain is also counted as a stitch.

Loop on hook

1 Make a foundation chain as long as you need. Half treble crochet begins with yrh, creating an extra loop, which adds height.

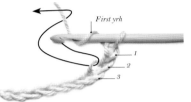

First yrh

1
2
3

2 Yrh, then insert the hook through the third chain from the hook and yrh again. The missed chains act like a turning chain (t-ch).

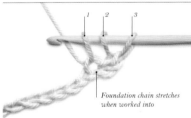

1 2 3

Foundation chain stretches when worked into

3 You now have three loops on the hook, with the yrh that you have done last being the loop closest to the tip.

Pull third yrh through all three loops

Turn lip downwards to avoid snagging

4 Yrh again and draw it through all three loops. This completes the first half treble stitch (htr).

5 Make htr stitches across the foundation chain. At the end of the row, turn your work, make a 2-chain t-ch, and work into the second stitch of the previous row to start the next row.

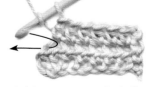

6 At the end of the next rows, work a half treble into the top of the turning chain from the previous row to keep the right number of stitches and your edges straight.

TREBLE CROCHET

38

Treble crochet is an attractive stitch that produces a softer, more open fabric – perfect for scarves and blankets. It is a tall stitch that works up quickly; treble crochet requires a 3-chain for turning.

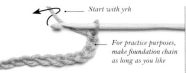

Start with yrh

For practice purposes, make foundation chain as long as you like

1 Make your foundation chain. Wrap your yarn around your hook before inserting it into the chain, as for half treble crochet.

First yrh

*1
2
3
4*

2 Insert the hook into the fourth chain from the hook. The three unused chains bring your work up to the correct height.

1 2 3

3 Yarn round hook again, then pull it through. You should now have three loops on your hook.

Pull hook through just first two loops

4 Yrh and draw it through the first two loops on your hook. This leaves you with two loops left on your hook.

Yrh, then pull through remaining loops

5 Yarn round hook again, and pull it through the remaining two loops. This is the finished treble stitch (tr).

Completed treble crochet stitch

Three missed chains at start of row

6 Keep working trebles into each foundation chain until the end. Turn your work and make a 3-chain t-ch to start the next row.

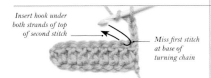

Insert hook under both strands of top of second stitch

Miss first stitch at base of turning chain

7 Miss the first stitch of the previous row. (Your t-ch counts as the first stitch in the new row.) Start each stitch with a yrh.

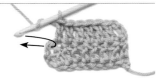

8 Continue to work trebles along the row with the last one worked into the top of the turning chain from the previous row.

39 DOUBLE TREBLE CROCHET

Double treble makes a loose, very soft fabric that is great for flowing, lacy wraps and baby blankets. Its extra height will make your work grow quickly and will be much lighter than double crochet.

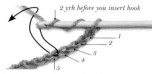

2 yrh before you insert hook

1 Make a foundation chain. Yrh twice, then insert it into the fifth chain from the hook. (The unused chains count as the first stitch.)

2 Yrh again and draw it through the chain. You now have four loops on your hook. Yrh and draw it through the first two loops.

3 There are now three loops on the hook. Yrh and draw it through the first two loops on your hook.

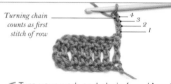

4 Only two loops remain on your hook. Yrh and draw it through these last two loops. This is the first double treble (dtr).

Completed dtr — *Four missed chains count as first stitch in row*

5 The four missed chain stitches form the first double treble stitch. Work a dtr stitch into each remaining foundation chain.

Turning chain counts as first stitch of row

6 Turn your work and chain four. (A pattern may tell you to chain then turn; whichever order you do it, the result is the same.)

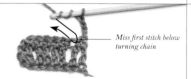

Miss first stitch below turning chain

7 Make your first dtr of this row in the top of the second stitch of the previous row. Your turning chain counts as the first stitch.

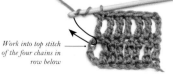

Work into top stitch of the four chains in row below

8 At the end of the row, work your final dtr into the top of the previous row's 4-chain. Go under both parts of the chain stitch's V.

STITCH HEIGHTS

40

This photo and diagram show how crochet stitches differ in height and how you can identify them. The diagram also indicates which foundation-chain stitch to insert your hook in to start each stitch, and how many turning chains are needed in each row. The longer the stitch, the quicker your work will grow, but it will also be looser and lacier. Think about the end use of your work when you are deciding which stitch will be best to use.

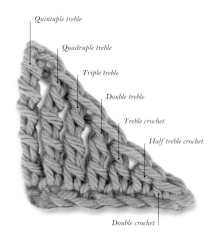

Quintuple treble

Quadruple treble

Triple treble

Double treble

Treble crochet

Half treble crochet

Double crochet

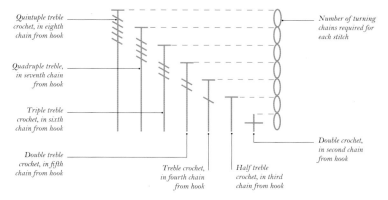

Quintuple treble crochet, in eighth chain from hook

Quadruple treble, in seventh chain from hook

Triple treble crochet, in sixth chain from hook

Double treble crochet, in fifth chain from hook

Treble crochet, in fourth chain from hook

Half treble crochet, in third chain from hook

Double crochet, in second chain from hook

Number of turning chains required for each stitch

RECOGNIZING STITCHES

41

It is useful to be able to recognize stitches by eye. If you make a mistake and don't wrap the yarn around the hook enough times on one stitch, you should be able to see quickly where the mistake was made, so you can rectify it. It can also help you work out which stitches you want to use in your work. Practise all the stitches and compare them so you can recognize them easily and see which ones you prefer.

42 TURNING CHAINS

When crocheting in rows, turning chains bring your hook up to the correct height to work the stitches. The chart on the right tells you how many chains to make at the start of rows for each crochet stitch. You will use starting chains when you crochet in the round, but the principle is exactly the same.

TURNING CHAINS FOR ROWS

Stitch	Number of turning chains needed
Double crochet	1
Half treble crochet	2
Treble crochet	3
Double treble crochet	4
Triple treble crochet	5

43 COUNTING STITCHES

If you are following a pattern and lose or gain stitches, it will greatly affect the finished piece. Keep track by counting the top Vs of each stitch. Check that your work is even and that there are no holes where stitches were missed, or dense areas with two stitches in one. Remember: you do not count the turning chain in double crochet as a stitch, but you do in the taller stitches.

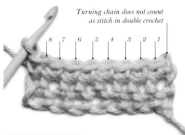

Turning chain does not count as stitch in double crochet

8 7 6 5 4 3 2 1

KEEP COUNTING
By counting the stitches, you can keep track of how many you have and thereby ensure you are following the pattern correctly.

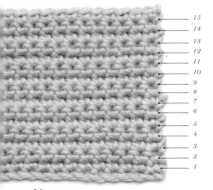

15
14
13
12
11
10
9
8
7
6
5
4
3
2
1

44 COUNTING ROWS

Just as you count stitches, so should you count rows – both to keep track of your pattern and to check tension (see Tip 19). Alternate rows look slightly different from each other because you turn the work when crocheting in rows. Being short, double crochet stitches are the hardest to count; with taller stitches, it is clearer to see where each row starts. Do not count the foundation chain as a row.

45 TRACKING STITCHES & ROWS

Get into the habit of counting your stitches at the end of each row to make sure you have the correct amount. Tracking is easy when working in back-and-forth-rows: just count stitches whenever you turn the work. Keep track of your rows, too – count them regularly or keep a tally chart on a piece of paper. Tracking is equally necessary when crocheting circles or tubes.

Use stitch marker or short piece of yarn in contrasting colour

KEEPING TRACK

A stitch marker is invaluable when working in the round or on tubes, so you know where one row finishes and the next should begin.

46 WHERE TO PUT YOUR HOOK

It is important to insert your hook into the correct place on the previous row when crocheting to get the desired affect and to maintain a neat, even finish. For all the basic stitches, you insert your hook under both arms of the V of the stitch you are working into. This gives a flat, uniform texture to your work. Patterns assume you will crochet this way and only give specific instructions if a different effect is required (see Tips 50 and 51).

LOOK FOR THE V

The two arms of the V are clearly visible in white yarn at the top of this photograph. This is the usual place for inserting your hook.

FINISHING OFF

47 When you have completed a piece you are working on, you must fasten off your work securely to prevent it from coming undone and all your efforts being lost. Whenever you finish off, be sure to leave a tail of about 10–15cm (4–6in) for weaving in.

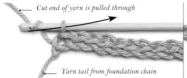

Cut end of yarn is pulled through

Yarn tail from foundation chain

Loop that was on hook, pulled out to prevent unravelling

Cut end is passed through loop that was on hook

FASTENING OFF WITH THE HOOK
Cut your yarn from the ball and pull the cut end through the loop using your hook. Pull the end of the yarn to tighten.

FASTENING OFF BY HAND
You do not have to use your hook to fasten off; you may do it by hand. Leave a long tail on the cut end to weave into your work.

SEWING IN ENDS

48 After finishing off (see Tip 47), weave the cut yarn into the main body of your work. This keeps it secure and creates a neat finish. You need a blunt-ended yarn needle with an eye large enough for your yarn. The most common methods are shown below.

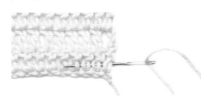

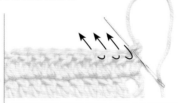

WEAVING THROUGH STITCHES
The easiest method is to weave about 10cm (4in) of yarn through the stitches, then cut the end as close to your work as possible.

WEAVING INTO THE TOP OF STITCHES
For a more secure finish, weave about 10cm (4in) of yarn into the top of the stitches in the final row, then cut close to your work.

UNDOING MISTAKES

49 The beauty of crochet is that it is easy to undo if you find you have gone wrong! Keeping track of your stitches and rows should mean you identify mistakes quickly and do not have to undo too much work. If you find a mistake, though, simply remove the hook and gently pull the yarn to undo one stitch at a time.

BACK LOOP ONLY

In crochet it is easy to achieve a ribbing effect. All you need to do is insert your hook under just the back loop (or arm) of the V, then work the stitch as normal. You can do this with a stitch of any height, but the longer stitches will give a wider ribbing effect.

Back loop only in double crochet

FOR A DEFINED RIB

Push your hook under the single strand at the back of the stitch for a ribbed effect that is more defined than regular crochet.

Front loop only in double crochet

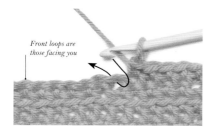

Front loops are those facing you

51 FRONT LOOP ONLY

Worked in a similar way to back loop only (see Tip 50), front loop only gives a less pronounced ribbing effect but still an attractive texture. To create it, insert your hook under the single loop at the front of the V of the stitch you are working into. Complete your stitch as normal. You can do this with any height of stitch. Experiment with combinations of back and front loop only to discover which effects are most pleasing to you.

A LESS OBVIOUS RIB

Insert your hook under the single strand at the front of the stitch you are working into.

52 JOINING A NEW YARN

As your crochet grows, you will need to work in extra balls of yarn. The best and neatest time to do this is at the beginning or end of a row. Check you have enough on your ball to finish your current row. You need long tails on both old and new yarns to weave them into your work.

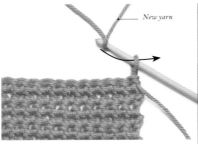

New yarn

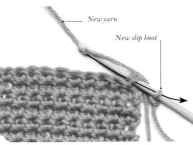

New yarn

New slip knot

METHOD 1
The easiest way is to drop the old yarn before you start the next row. Pull the new yarn through the loop, and work across the row as usual. Weave in the ends later.

METHOD 2
Fasten off the old yarn, and attach the new yarn to the hook with a slip knot. Insert the hook into the first stitch of the row, yrh, and pull through both loops on the hook.

53 CHANGING COLOURS

A new colour will usually be added at the end of a row, for a neat, seamless join. Mostly, you will use yarns of the same weight and fibre content to ensure a uniform finish and the same cleaning instructions. However, if you experiment with different textures and weights, be aware of the stresses this will put on the finished fabric.

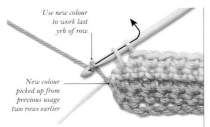

Use new colour to work last yrh of row

New colour picked up from previous usage two rows earlier

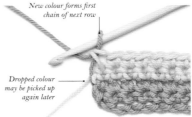

New colour forms first chain of next row

Dropped colour may be picked up again later

1 For the last stitch in the row of the old colour, make the last yrh with the new colour that is to be used in the next row.

2 Draw the new colour through the last yrh in the previous row's final stitch, and use it to make the turning chain of the next row.

54 WORKING BETWEEN STITCHES

When you have mastered basic stitches and feel confident in creating even fabrics, experiment with different methods to achieve new textures – if using tall stitches, work the next row between the stitches, for example, rather than into the top of them. This creates a lovely open texture and makes it easier to use very fluffy yarns such as alpaca, since you can clearly see where to put your hook.

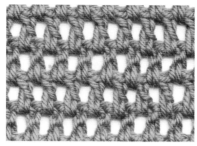

Treble crochet worked between stitches

CREATING A NEW TEXTURE

Instead of inserting your hook under the top V of a stitch, put it between the stitches, right under the whole of the top of the stitch.

55 WORKING INTO A CHAIN SPACE

Many patterns add chain stitches between the main crochet stitches to create an open texture. Short lengths are called chain spaces, and long lengths worked into a row are called loops. Chain spaces can create interesting textures and designs. When you work into chain spaces or loops, be sure to go under the chain rather than through the stitches themselves.

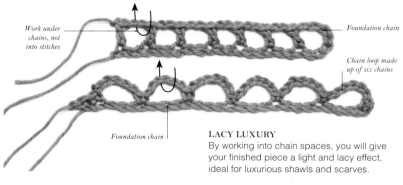

Work under chains, not into stitches

Foundation chain

Chain loop made up of six chains

Foundation chain

LACY LUXURY

By working into chain spaces, you will give your finished piece a light and lacy effect, ideal for luxurious shawls and scarves.

56 KEEPING YOUR WORK STRAIGHT

If you find that the edges of your work aren't square, you may have missed working into either the first or last stitches of a row. Remember to make a turning chain of appropriate length at the start of a row, and always work the first stitch into the correct stitch of the previous row. At the end of the row, work into the last stitch or top of the chain of the previous row.

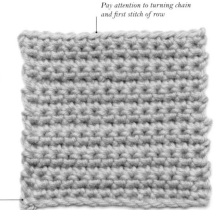

Pay attention to turning chain and first stitch of row

In dc, don't miss last stitch from previous row

57 INCREASING & DECREASING

To create different shapes, you must learn how to make your crochet wider or narrower as required. This is called increasing and decreasing. You add stitches to the row to increase, and you work stitches together to decrease. A pattern will tell you when to do it and by how many stitches. Increases and decreases are usually distributed evenly to ensure a smooth line.

INCREASE YOUR RANGE

By mastering increases and decreases, you will extend the range of things you can make. Garments, toys, and accessories often require you to change the number of stitches in a row, so it is worth knowing how.

58 DOUBLE CROCHET INCREASE

Increasing makes your work wider. It is normally done in pairs, with one increase at the beginning of the row and one at the end, to keep your work even. It is very simple – you just work two stitches in the same place. To increase a piece of double crochet, work your first dc as normal, then work another in the same place. Do the same at the end of the row, and you have increased your stitch count by two. A pattern will tell you how many stitches you should have after any increases so you can double-check the row.

Completed first dc

2 dc worked into same stitch

1 To increase at the beginning of the row, start by completing one dc as normal in the first stitch.

2 Next, insert your hook into the same place and work another dc stitch. This is your first increase.

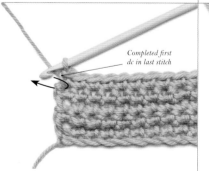

Completed first dc in last stitch

2 dc worked into same stitch

3 Work the rest of the row as usual until you reach the end. At the end of the row, make one dc in the last stitch as normal.

4 Now insert your hook into the same place again and make another dc. This is your second increase in the row.

43

DOUBLE CROCHET DECREASE

59 Decreasing the number of stitches in a row makes your work narrower. Like increasing, this is usually done in pairs to keep the work even. To decrease, you merge stitches together on the last yrh. A pattern will tell you when to decrease and by how many stitches. It will also tell you how many stitches you should have so you can check your work.

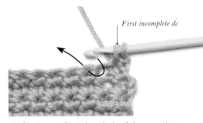

First incomplete dc

1 Start your first dc stitch of the row, but stop before you complete the last yrh. You will have two loops on your hook. Insert the hook into the next stitch, and draw up a loop.

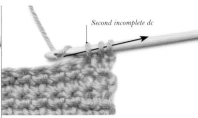

Second incomplete dc

2 You should now have three loops on your hook. Wrap the yarn around the hook, then draw it through all three loops on your hook.

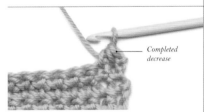

Completed decrease

3 You have now completed your first decrease. In fact, you have merged two stitches into one, known as dc2tog.

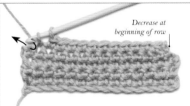

Decrease at beginning of row

4 Work the rest of the row normally, until you have two stitches left. Put your hook in the second-to-last stitch and draw through a loop.

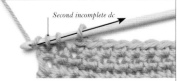

Second incomplete dc

5 You now have two loops on your hook. Insert the hook through the last stitch of the row, and draw a loop through. You should now have three loops on your hook.

Completed decrease

6 Yrh, and pull through all three loops on your hook. You have merged two stitches into one and should now have two stitches fewer in this row than in the previous one.

60

DOUBLE CROCHET THREE TOGETHER DECREASE

Abbreviated to dc3tog, this is a way of decreasing by two stitches at the same time. It gives a sharper decreasing shape to your finished piece. You simply work three incomplete dc, stopping before the last yrh, then join them together with the final yrh on the last stitch. Essentially, what this means is that you combine three stitches into one.

61

TREBLE CROCHET INCREASE

As in double crochet, treble crochet increases are usually worked in pairs, one at each end of a row. Treble crochet increasing also works for the other tall stitches. If you work a treble (or taller stitch) into the first stitch, instead of missing it in the normal way, you will increase by one stitch at the start of the row. At the end of the row, work two stitches together into the top of the previous row's turning chain.

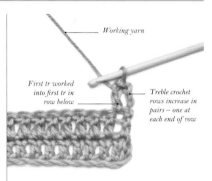

Working yarn

First tr worked into first tr in row below

Treble crochet rows increase in pairs – one at each end of row

1 Instead of missing the first treble of the row below, work a treble into it to increase by one stitch at the start of the row.

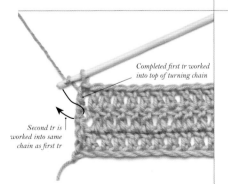

Completed first tr worked into top of turning chain

Second tr is worked into same chain as first tr

2 At the end of the row, work a treble into the top of the turning chain in the row below as usual.

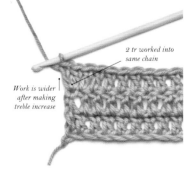

2 tr worked into same chain

Work is wider after making treble increase

3 Work another treble into the same place at the top of the turning chain on the row below. The row has increased by two stitches.

62 TREBLE CROCHET DECREASE

Treble crochet decreasing will make your work narrower. It is important to know how to shape your work this way because you will need to do it when making garments and other projects. Your pattern will tell you when to decrease and by how many stitches. Decreasing stitches at the beginning and end of a row is called external decreasing; if done in the middle, it is called internal decreasing.

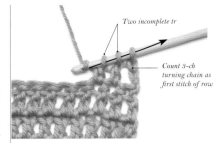

Two incomplete tr

Count 3-ch turning chain as first stitch of row

1 Make the turning chain. Miss the first tr of the previous row, then work a tr into the next two stitches up to the last yrh of each. You now have three loops on your hook.

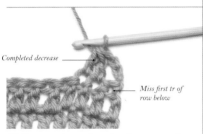

Completed decrease

Miss first tr of row below

2 Once you have drawn up the yarn and passed it through all three loops, you have completed your first treble decrease. You have combined two stitches into one.

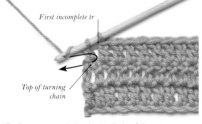

First incomplete tr

Top of turning chain

3 As you reach the last stitch of the row below, work one tr up to the last yrh (first incomplete tr). Work another incomplete tr in the top of the previous row's turning chain.

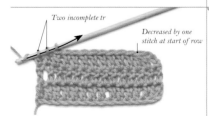

Two incomplete tr

Decreased by one stitch at start of row

4 You should now have three loops on your hook. Yarn round hook, and draw through all three loops.

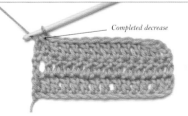

Completed decrease

5 The end-of-row decrease is completed. You can use the same method to work three stitches together to decrease by two stitches at a time instead of one.

WORKING IN THE ROUND

MAGIC ADJUSTABLE RING

63 Working in circles adds a whole new dimension to your work. You can make toys, flowers, bowls, and a range of shapes, such as granny squares that can be sewn together to make blankets. Many patterns will require you to know how to do it. Instead of a foundation chain, you make a circle of stitches; the magic adjustable ring is a good way to start.

1 Make a circle with your yarn, and draw the yarn through so that it forms a loose loop round your hook.

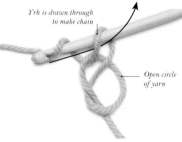

Yrh is drawn through to make chain

Open circle of yarn

2 Keep the circle open, then yrh and pull through the loop to make a chain stitch. Make as many chains as you require.

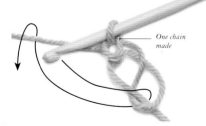

One chain made

3 Make your first round of stitches into the circle, crocheting over the loose tail. (The example shown uses double crochet.)

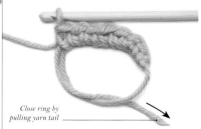

Close ring by pulling yarn tail

4 Make the required number of stitches into the circle, and pull the tail of the yarn to close the ring. Then go on with the pattern.

CHAIN CIRCLE

64 Another way to start work in the round is by using a chain circle. However, this can be more fiddly than a magic adjustable ring because it doesn't expand to accommodate your stitches and sometimes leaves a larger hole in the middle. You may find that you have to move the stitches made previously out of the way so you can carry on making the required amount of stitches into the chain circle.

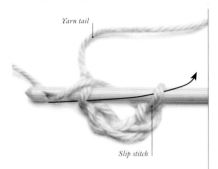

Yarn tail

Slip stitch

One chain

Work stitches over yarn tail

1 Chain as many stitches as your pattern requires. In the example shown here, it is a 4-chain. Join the first and last chain together with a slip stitch.

2 To start working into the ring, make as many chains as your stitch height requires. This example is double crochet, so it is one chain.

Tighten ring by pulling yarn tail

Safety pin used as stitch marker

Safety pin is moved to last stitch at end of each round

3 Work as many stitches into the circle as you need, crocheting over the yarn tail to secure it. Use a stitch marker or safety pin to mark the final stitch of the ring.

4 To make the flat circle shape, you need to work 2 dc into each stitch of the first round. These extra stitches create the circle's curved edge.

WORKING IN ROWS

65

When working in the round, you can work in separate rows or crochet in a continuous spiral. Crocheting in rows gives definition to each round and enables neat colour changes (which can look jagged in a spiral). To work rows in the round, join the last stitch of the round to the first with a slip stitch. Then make a chain as high as your stitches require (see Tip 40).

CROCHETING ROWS IN THE ROUND
Use a stitch marker to indicate where the first stitch of each round is. Join rounds at the top of the chain with a slip stitch.

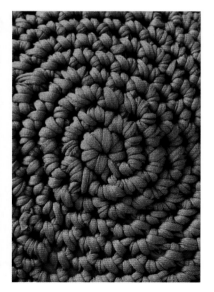

WORKING IN A SPIRAL

66

It is possible to crochet a flat circle in one continuous spiral. You need to know how many stitches should be in each round, and mark the first one with a stitch marker. Then, instead of joining up the round with a slip stitch, just keep crocheting. You don't have to worry about starting chains, since you are working outwards all the time. Remember to increase your stitches in each round to keep the work flat and to make it into a circle shape (see Tip 67).

ROUND AND ROUND
You don't join the rounds when working in a spiral, but you do need to move your stitch marker to the first stitch of each new round.

49

INCREASING IN A CIRCLE

To make a circle, you must increase the number of stitches in each round. The first round is worked into the ring; the next round is usually two stitches into each of the first round, doubling the number of stitches. The following rounds usually space the increases gradually further apart. For instance, in round three, make one normal stitch between increases; in round four, make two normal stitches between increases; and so on.

EVEN INCREASING

To make a flat round shape, you must increase your stitches evenly. Most patterns will tell you how and where to make the increases.

KEEPING YOUR CIRCLE FLAT

Sometimes, when you crochet a flat circle, you may find that the edges become wavy. This may be because you have made too many or too few increases, or made them unevenly around the circle. It is best to undo it and start again, keeping track of how many increases you make. Your pattern should tell you.

ROUND & FLAT

Increase by the correct amount each time, and keep the increases evenly spaced around the circle to keep your work flat.

AMIGURUMI

WHAT IS AMIGURUMI?

Amigurumi is Japanese for "small stuffed doll", but it is now widely used for any small crocheted toy. The patterns are usually quick and easy to crochet, and the end results are great presents for children. Use a tough, washable yarn and a hook slightly smaller than the yarn recommends, for a firm tension.

CROCHETED CRITTERS
Once you've mastered the basics of amigurumi, you can experiment with making your own designs.

70 3D SHAPES

In crochet, it is easy to make three-dimensional shapes with little or no sewing. You can use double crochet stitches to create firm tubes, balls, and ovals, which are the basis for most amigurumi. If you start making a flat circle but stop increasing the stitches as you work, the edges will rise up like walls. Double crochet creates a dense, stiff fabric that is especially suited to amigurumi.

SEW EASY!
The only sewing required for amigurumi is to stitch the component crocheted parts together – the legs to the body, for example.

51

71

BALLS

A ball or sphere is a useful three-dimensional shape to master. Not only do balls make great baby gifts, but you can use the technique to make other things, such as heads for toys. The pattern opposite is for the centre-striped ball shown below. You can change the yarn colour after every round to make the all-over striped ball. Once you are comfortable with making balls, try out different sizes and colours.

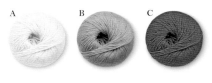

WHAT YOU NEED

You can use any yarn, but 4-ply mercerized cotton is a great way to start. Use as many or as few colours as you like. You also need a slightly smaller hook than normal – a 2mm will give a tighter tension.

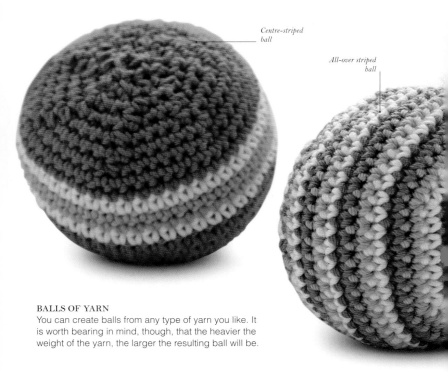

Centre-striped ball

All-over striped ball

BALLS OF YARN

You can create balls from any type of yarn you like. It is worth bearing in mind, though, that the heavier the weight of the yarn, the larger the resulting ball will be.

Tricoloured ball

OFFSET SEAM

An offset seam will form on the striped ball as a result of the spiral method of working in rounds (see Tips 65 and 66).

PATTERN INSTRUCTIONS

Start with your main colour (C). Work 6 dc into a magic adjustable ring. Pull the yarn tail to close it tightly.

Round 1: 2 dc in each dc around to end (12 sts).

Round 2: * 1 dc in next dc, 2 dc in next dc; rep from * to end (18 sts).

Round 3: * 1 dc in next 2 dc, 2 dc in next dc; rep from * to end (24 sts).

Round 4: * 1 dc in next 3 dc, 2 dc in next dc; rep from* to end (30 sts).

Round 5: * 1 dc in next 4 dc, 2 dc in next dc; rep from * to end (36 sts).

Round 6: * 1 dc in next 5 dc, 2 dc in next dc; rep from * to end (42 sts).

Round 7: * 1 dc in next 6 dc, 2 dc in next dc; rep from * to end (48 sts).

Rounds 8 & 9:1 dc in each dc around; finish last yrh with second colour, yarn A.

Round 10: with yarn A, work 1 dc in each dc to end; finish last yrh with third colour, yarn B.

Rounds 11 & 12: with yarn B, work 1 dc in each dc around; finish last yrh with yarn A.

Round 13: with yarn A, work 1 dc in each dc around; finish last yrh with yarn C.

Rounds 14 & 15: with yarn C, work 1 dc in each dc around.

Round 16: * 1 dc in each of the next 6 dc, dc2tog; rep from * to end (42 sts).

Round 17: * 1 dc in each of the next 5 dc, dc2tog; rep from * to end (36 sts).

Round 18: * 1 dc in each of the next 4 dc, dc2tog; rep from * to end (30 sts).

Round 19: * 1 dc in each of the next 3 dc; dc2tog; rep from * to end (24 sts).

Round 20: * 1 dc in each of the next 2 dc; dc2tog; rep from * to end (18 sts).

Round 21: * 1 dc in the next dc, dc2tog; rep from * to end (12 sts). Stuff very firmly (see Tip 73).

Round 22: dc2tog to end (6sts). Fasten off, leaving a long tail to weave in to close the hole.

Weave in yarn tail from the initial magic adjustable ring.

72 INVISIBLE DECREASE

When you decrease by one stitch (dc2tog) or two (dc3tog), you can make it less obvious by using the invisible decrease, a method that works particularly well in the round. The principle is the same as a normal decrease, but you insert your hook under the front loops only of the stitches you are working together. This means there is less bulk in the stitch, since only half the amount of yarn is gathered up.

73 STUFFING

It is best to use stuffing that is washable and hypo-allergenic. For toys, check the stuffing is safe for children. It is always best to stuff your piece firmly when it's near completion. The stuffing will flatten with use, but be careful not to overstuff, since this may stretch and distort your stitches.

Finished item should be firmly stuffed

TAKING SHAPE

The stuffing will give shape to your work. You should not be able to see the stuffing once you have finished the item and closed up the hole.

74 SEWING TOGETHER

To ensure your hard work isn't easily undone, use a blunt-ended yarn needle to sew in the yarn tail when you have finished stuffing your piece. Weave the yarn in and out of the last stitches so no hole remains from which the stuffing can leak out. Weave the rest of the yarn tail around the end of the work to hide it and create a more secure finish.

Weave through stitches, and pull hole closed

HOLD TIGHT

Weave in yarn tails firmly to prevent toys from unravelling when they are played with. Once done, cut the yarn as close to the work as possible.

TUBES

75

Learning to crochet tubes is useful, since they are used in everything from toys, to socks, to gloves. Like circles, tubes can be worked in spirals or rows. When working in rows you can also turn your work (as you would a square piece of crochet) to get a different pattern effect. The steps below show you how to work treble crochet in rows without turning to form a tube.

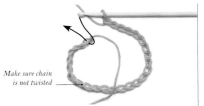

Make sure chain is not twisted

1 Make a chain the length you need; this will be the diameter of the finished tube. Join the ends with a slip stitch to form a ring.

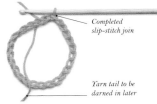

Completed slip-stitch join

Yarn tail to be darned in later

2 Unlike a circle, the stitches are worked into the chain stitches, not around them. Leave a long tail to be woven in at the end.

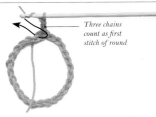

Three chains count as first stitch of round

3 Chain 3 to begin the first round of treble crochet. Make one tr in each chain. Don't twist the chain; the right side should face you.

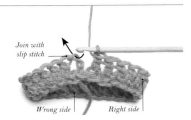

Join with slip stitch

Wrong side   *Right side*

4 At the end of the round, join the last stitch to the top of the turning chain using a slip stitch. Ensure your stitch count is correct.

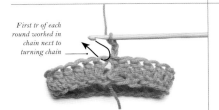

First tr of each round worked in chain next to turning chain

5 Start the second round with a turning chain of three chains. (Remember not to turn the work, despite having a turning chain.)

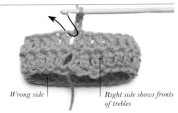

Wrong side   *Right side shows fronts of trebles*

6 The turning chain counts as the first stitch, so start your trebles from the next stitch along. Continue this way for the tube's length.

76 TENSION

When you are making amigurumi items such as toys and balls, it is best to work in double crochet with a smaller hook size than normal. The size of the hook affects the tension of your work, and items that are to be stuffed and played with need a denser, tighter tension in the fabric. The important thing to remember is to go a size smaller on your hook but to stick to your usual crochet style. This will create the stronger, denser fabric that will hold the stuffing in place and withstand the stresses of child's play.

WEIGHT & SIZE
Yarn weight affects the size of a finished item. A doll made in chunky yarn will be bigger than one made in 4-ply to the same pattern.

Amigurumi rabbit

PLAY SAFE
Children put toys through their paces, as well as in their mouths, so aim for a durable finished item made of all non-toxic materials.

77 OTHER ACCESSORIES

Once you have begun making amigurumi, you will need some extra bits to complete them. You can embroider eyes and noses on to your creations, but you can also purchase plastic safety pieces, which are especially designed to be safe for children. Such items have a washer at the back that is pressed firmly on to the stalk of the eye and prevents them from being pulled off.

Safety back pieces in various sizes

Safety nose

Ribbon for use as collars

Brown eyes

Blue eyes

Wide ribbon

Child-safe stuffing

WORKING WITH GARMENTS

78 SEAMS

When you make clothing, you join together the separate elements using seams. The pattern will tell you where to join them. Several techniques are shown here; use the most appropriate seam for the garment, and align your pieces correctly. Patterns refer to right side (RS) for the side that will be on display, and wrong side (WS) for the other side.

79 MATTRESS STITCH

This stitch makes a flat, neat seam in any type of crochet stitch. Use a length of the same yarn as your main crochet and a blunt-ended needle. Here we have used a contrasting colour to illustrate the technique more clearly.

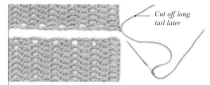

Cut off long tail later

1 Place your crochet pieces right side up, with the row ends together. Insert your needle through the corner of the top piece.

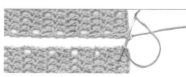

2 Secure the yarn by making two or three stitches into the first crochet stitches of the seam.

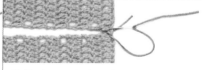

3 Put the needle through the stitches at the edge of your crochet on one side and then the other, working pairs of small stitches.

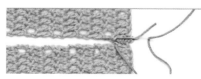

4 Continue to make small stitches in alternation through the crochet stitches at the edge of each side of your crochet.

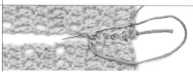

5 Pull the yarn tight as you go to close the seam and hide the stitches. Secure the yarn at the end, and weave in the tails.

80

WHIP STITCH

The whip stitch, or overcast stitch, creates a strong seam with a slight ridge on the wrong side. The small, neat stitches are worked in a spiral over the two sides of your crochet.

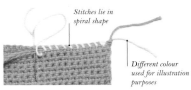

Stitches lie in spiral shape

Different colour used for illustration purposes

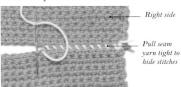

Right side

Pull seam yarn tight to hide stitches

SIMPLE WHIP STITCH
Place your crochet pieces one on top of the other, right sides together, and secure the yarn. Stitch through both layers of crochet.

FLAT WHIP STITCH
For a flat seam, place the pieces right side up, edge to edge. Work the whip stitch (see left) but through the crochet's back loop only.

81

BACKSTITCH

Backstitch creates a strong seam that is great for garments. Place your crochet pieces with right sides together, and secure the first corner with two or three whip stitches.

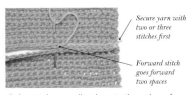

Secure yarn with two or three stitches first

Forward stitch goes forward two spaces

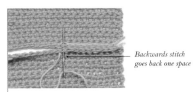

Backwards stitch goes back one space

1 Insert the needle close to the edge of your crochet, and sew through both pieces. Skip one stitch, then insert your needle again.

2 Next, work a stitch back into the stitch missed by the forward stitch. This helps make the seam especially strong.

82

SLIP STITCH

This compact seam is worked with a crochet hook rather than a yarn needle. Place the right sides together, then, with a new piece of yarn attached with a slip knot, insert the hook under the back loops only of the two layers, yrh, and pull through to slip stitch. Fasten off as usual, and sew in the tail ends.

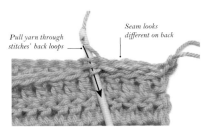

Pull yarn through stitches' back loops

Seam looks different on back

Slip stitch highlighted with contrasting yarn

83 FRONT POST CROCHET

When using taller stitches such as treble crochet, there is room to work the hook around the "post" of the next stitch instead of into the top loop. If you are working in rows, this technique of working around the post produces a ribbing effect by creating ridges in the fabric.

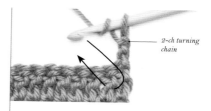

2-ch turning chain

1 Crochet a row of treble stitches. Chain 2, yrh, and insert the hook from the front, right to left, around the post of the second treble.

2 Next, yrh and pull the loop through, then yrh and pull through first two loops on the hook twice. This completes the treble.

Ridge forms behind front post trebles

3 Continue across the row. Finish with a half treble into the top of the turning chain. Repeat until the required length.

84 BACK POST CROCHET

This stitch is essentially the same as in Tip 83, but with the hook going in from behind. In both back and front post stitches, the stitch height is lower than normal, so it needs a shorter turning chain. In each, you only need a 2-chain turning, and the row ends in a half treble.

2-ch turning chain

1 Start with a row of trebles. Chain 2, yrh, and insert the hook from the back, right to left, around the post of the next stitch.

2 Next, yrh and pull the loop through, then yrh and pull through first two loops on the hook twice. This completes the treble.

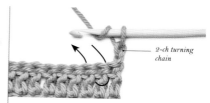

Ridge forms at front of back post trebles

3 Continue across the row. Finish with a half treble into the top of the turning chain. Repeat until the required length.

SEWN-ON EDGING

85

Edging your work gives it a decorative, professional finish. You can add edging either by creating an additional piece and sewing it on to your work or by crocheting it directly on to the item (see Tip 86). To sew on an edge, use a blunt-ended needle and a yarn that matches the main work.

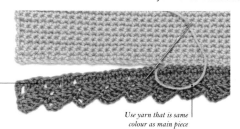

Be sure to sew edging on the right way around

Use yarn that is same colour as main piece

PUTTING IT ALL TOGETHER
Sew on the edging with overcast stitches evenly spaced along the work. Finish off the ends neatly.

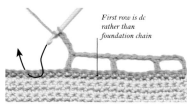

First row is dc rather than foundation chain

1 Start by making a row of double crochet along your main piece. Once you get to the end, turn your work and begin your edging pattern.

CROCHETED-ON EDGING

86

It is important to remember that if you are adding a decorative edge directly on to your work, you must make sure that the pattern you use for the edging will work with the number of stitches in your main piece.

2 At the end of the row, turn your work again and continue with the pattern. Repeat until the edge is completed.

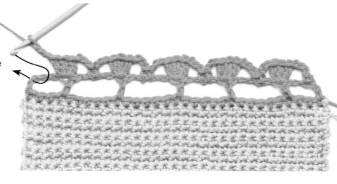

GRANNY SQUARES

87

WHAT IS A GRANNY SQUARE?

The ever-popular, lacy-looking granny squares are versatile and fun to make. Although square, they are actually made in the round. You can use almost any tall stitches, and by combining different colours you can make bags, blankets, or cardigans. Granny squares are a great way to use up leftover yarn, too. The size of the square is up to you too; just keep adding more rounds.

A three-round granny square

88

BASIC GRANNY SQUARE

In a granny square, the pattern repeats around a ring, and the corners are usually squared off with increases. The basic granny square is formed of grouped trebles and chain spaces. You will soon pick up how the pattern works, which makes for a relaxing project to work on.

Working yarn

Bring yarn tail closer to ring to stitch over it later

1 Chain 6, and join them into a ring with a slip stitch.

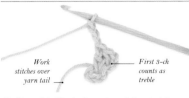

Work stitches over yarn tail

First 3-ch counts as treble

2 Round 1. Chain 3, and work two trebles into the ring. Chain 3 again. Make three trebles into the ring; and chain 3; repeat twice.

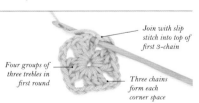

Join with slip stitch into top of first 3-chain

Four groups of three trebles in first round

Three chains form each corner space

3 Finish the round with a slip stitch into the top of the first 3-ch. Pull the starting tail of the yarn to tighten up the centre ring.

89 CORNERS

Keeping the corners square is what gives the granny square its shape, and this is done by increasing stitches. This is also a good place to start using a new colour (see Tip 90).

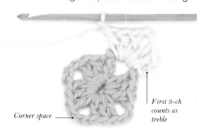

Corner space

First 3-ch counts as treble

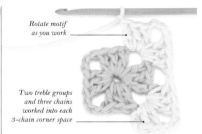

Rotate motif as you work

Two treble groups and three chains worked into each 3-chain corner space

1 Round 2. Chain 3, and work two trebles, three chains, and three trebles into the first corner of round one. The first chain counts as a treble.

2 Chain 1, and work three trebles, three chains, and three trebles into the next corner space; do this three times, then join the top of the first 3-ch with a slip stitch.

---

90 JOINING NEW COLOURS

It is easy to join new colours when making granny squares. Make sure you start a new colour in the corner spaces. If you are changing colours more than once, make sure you use a different corner each time, otherwise your work will be distorted in one corner as you crochet over the yarn ends.

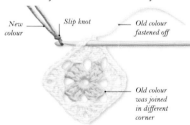

New colour

Slip knot

Old colour fastened off

Old colour was joined in different corner

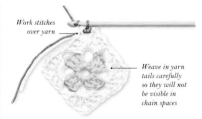

Work stitches over yarn

Weave in yarn tails carefully so they will not be visible in chain spaces

1 Fasten off the old colour, and leave a tail to crochet over. Put the new colour on the hook using a slip knot, and insert the hook into one of the corner spaces. Yrh, and pull through the loop on the hook. This joins the new colour securely.

2 Make the correct number of chains – three for this pattern, for example – and continue to complete the round as shown, making sure you crochet over both of the yarn tails. This saves the need for weaving them in later.

91 JOINING TOGETHER

The beauty of granny squares is that you can make them as big or small as you like. You can even combine squares of different sizes into the same piece of work. It is important that they are joined together well, since this will make the finished item more durable. There are several methods, but two of the most common are shown below.

FLAT SLIP-STITCH SEAM
Place the motifs right side up, and work slip stitches through the back loop of the top of each stitch along the seam.

DOUBLE CROCHET SEAM
Place the pieces right sides together, and double crochet along the seam through the back loops only of each stitch.

92 OTHER MOTIFS

Once you start to explore crochet patterns, you'll find a vast range of different motifs – individual blocks of crochet that are joined together to form larger pieces or used as decorative patches. They are usually based on a repeating pattern and are fun and easy to make. When you have mastered a few, you will find that you won't need to keep referring to the pattern.

PLAIN SQUARE
This square is formed of trebles with chain spaces at the corners.

SIMPLE HEXAGON
Hexagons fit together beautifully to create blankets with a more interesting look.

FLOWER HEXAGON
This pretty and easy-to-make variation incorporates bobbles (see Tip 98) to add texture.

93

WHY BLOCK?

Blocking is a way of making your finished crochet the correct size and shape, since it may distort as you work on it. This is especially important when sewing together pieces that need to be the same size. Check your yarn's care instructions before you begin, especially when using delicate yarns, to ensure you use the method most suitable for your work.

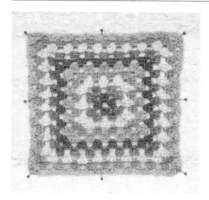

94

WET BLOCKING

This method gives the best results – as long as your yarn can be washed. Wet the pieces thoroughly in warm water, and roll them in a clean towel to squeeze out any excess. Using layers of towels covered by a colour-safe sheet, pin your pieces into shape right side down. Allow them to dry completely.

PIN IT DOWN
Use as many sewing pins as necessary to keep your crochet in the correct shape.

95

STEAM BLOCKING

Steam blocking is a quicker method than wet blocking. Again, check that your yarn is suitable for this method, then pin the piece out, right side down. Place a clean, damp cloth over the crochet, and very lightly steam each piece with an iron. Allow the pieces to dry fully before unpinning them.

IRON CAREFULLY
Never let the iron rest on the crochet, since it will flatten the texture.

WORKING STITCHES TOGETHER

96 CLUSTERS

Beautiful effects can be achieved by grouping and merging stitches. A cluster is one such combined stitch. Clusters are made by joining several stitches at the top to form one stitch, and they add great texture and interest to your crochet. Any stitch from half treble upwards can be made to form clusters.

1 To make a three-treble cluster, insert the hook where your pattern instructs, and work a treble up until the last yrh (an incomplete tr). Then work incomplete trebles into the next two stitches. This will leave you with four loops on your hook.

2 Wrap the yarn around the hook, and draw through all four loops on the hook. This completes all three trebles and merges them into one stitch.

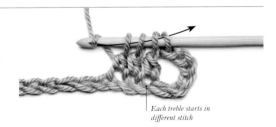

Each treble starts in different stitch

3 You now have a three-treble cluster. It is possible to make clusters with as many stitches as you like. Experiment with them to see the different effects.

Top of cluster becomes single stitch

97 SHELLS

These stitch groupings resemble upside-down clusters. They are usually worked with trebles and are very easy to master. Shells are a very popular stitch, and you simply work several stitches into one stitch to form a pattern. Like clusters, shells can be made with any number or height of stitch, from half treble upwards.

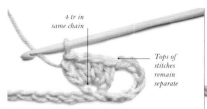

4 tr in same chain

Tops of stitches remain separate

5 tr in same chain

Tops of stitches remain separate

FOUR-TREBLE SHELL
Work four trebles into the same chain space or stitch. Skip the next two stitches to allow room for the additional stitches in the shell.

FIVE-TREBLE SHELL
As with clusters, you can work as many trebles as you like to make a shell, but more than six may distort the line of your crochet.

98 BOBBLES

A bobble is a combination of clusters and shells. They are a little raised and give a nice visual effect and texture. Although they look complicated, they are very easy to make. You can use as many stitches as you like to create a bobble, and they are usually worked in half treble or taller.

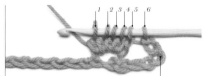

1 2 3 4 5 6

See pattern for how many chains to miss at beginning

1 Work the first treble until you reach the last yrh, but don't complete it. Repeat this process until you have six loops on the hook.

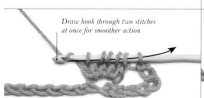

Draw hook through two stitches at once for smoother action

2 Yrh, and draw through all six loops. You may need to draw the hook through two stitches at a time to prevent snagging.

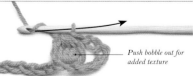

Push bobble out for added texture

3 The completed bobble can be pushed inwards or outwards in the centre to give more texture to the piece.

67

99 PICOT STITCHES

These small chain rings give a pretty texture to your crochet. They are created by joining a few chain stitches into a loop using slip stitch. They can be used for edging or combined with other stitches to create a wide range of interesting effects.

Completed picot stitch

Use slip stitch to close picot

1 In this pattern, work four chains and close the picot with a slip stitch into the fourth chain from the hook.

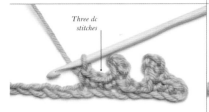

Three dc stitches

2 Work three double crochet stitches in between each picot to keep the spacing correct for the pattern.

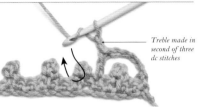

Treble made in second of three dc stitches

3 After the picot row, work a 2-ch space above each picot and a tr between them. Repeat alternating rows for a mesh design.

100 FILET CROCHET

This lacy, open style uses chains and trebles to create a grid of stitches. To make a pattern, some of the squares are filled in with trebles. Filet is usually worked in finer yarns and is made by following a chart such as the one below.

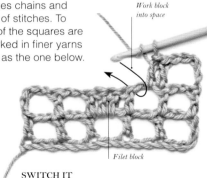

Work block into space

Filet block

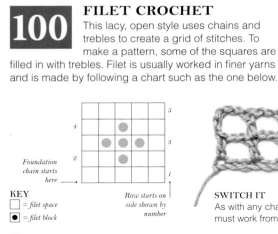

Foundation chain starts here

Row starts on side shown by number

KEY

☐ = *filet space*

⬤ = *filet block*

SWITCH IT
As with any chart, left-handed crocheters must work from a mirror image.

OTHER TYPES OF CROCHET

101

Now you have mastered traditional crochet and are having fun creating your own clothes, toys, and home furnishings, why not experiment with some variations of this craft? Based on the same principles, the crochet types shown below give different results. Information and patterns are readily available for these techniques, and they will all add to your repertoire of crochet skills.

BROOMSTICK CROCHET
In this variant, a large thick stick holds the stitches (see above) as you crochet with a normal hook, creating an attractive looped effect (see right).

IRISH CROCHET
This technique was developed to mimic lace. It is usually worked in fine cottons and often uses flower motifs to create beautiful fabrics.

TUNISIAN, OR AFGHAN, CROCHET
A long hook is used in this technique, and the stitches stay on the hook as you work the row. It is ideal for making dense, warm fabrics.

INDEX

ACKNOWLEDGMENTS

Sands Publishing Solutions would like to thank
Lucy Horne for being so easy-going and patient when faced with those
of us new to crocheting; Tia Sarkar at DK for her helpful crochet-specific
editorial input; Natalie Godwin for design assistance; and the ever-brilliant
Hilary Bird for making such swift work of the index.

Dorling Kindersley would like to thank the following photographers:
Deepak Aggarwal, Peter Anderson, Ruth Jenkinson, Dave King, Simon Murrell.

Picture credits
All images © Dorling Kindersley.
For further information, see www.dkimages.com